Pablo Picasso
Master of Modern Art

Liz Gogerly

Raintree
Chicago, Illinois

Titles in this series:
Muhammad Ali: The Greatest—Neil Armstrong: The First Man on the Moon—Fidel Castro: Leader of Cuba's Revolution—Roald Dahl: The Storyteller—The Dalai Lama: Peacemaker from Tibet——Anne Frank: Voice of Hope—Mahatma Gandhi: The Peaceful Revolutionary—Bill Gates: Computer Legend—Martin Luther King, Jr.: Civil Rights Hero—John Lennon: Musician with a Message—Nelson Mandela: Father of Freedom—Wolfgang Amadeus Mozart: Musical Genius—Florence Nightingale: The Lady of the Lamp—Pope John Paul II: Pope for the People—Pablo Picasso: Master of Modern Art—Elvis Presley: The King of Rock and Roll—Queen Elizabeth II: Monarch of Our Times—The Queen Mother: Grandmother of a Nation—William Shakespeare: Poet and Playwright—Vincent Van Gogh: The Troubled Artist

© 2004 Raintree
Published by Raintree, a division of Reed Elsevier, Inc.
Chicago, Illinois
Customer Service 888-363-4266
Visit our website at www.raintreelibrary.com

Printed in Hong Kong.
07 06 05 04 03
10 9 8 7 6 5 4 3 2 1

Library of Congress Cataloging in Publication Data
Gogerly, Liz.
   Pablo Picasso / Liz Gogerly.
      p. cm. -- (Famous lives)
Summary: Introduces the life and work of artist Pablo Picasso, whofounded the movement known as Cubism. Includes bibliographical references and index.
   ISBN 0-7398-6628-1 (library binding : hardcover)
   1. Picasso, Pablo, 1881-1973--Juvenile literature. 2. Artists--France--Biography--Juvenile literature. [1. Picasso, Pablo,1881-1973. 2. Artists. 3. Painting, French. 4. Painting, Modern--20th century.] I. Picasso, Pablo, 1881-1973. II. Title. III. Series: Famous lives (Chicago, Ill.)
   N6853.P5G63 2004
   709'.2--dc21
                          2003006106

Picture acknowledgments
The publisher would like to thank the following for permission to reproduce photographs:
pp. 4, 7, 26, 41, 42, 45 Camera Press; pp. 5, 8, 9, 18, 22, 29, 35, 37, 43, 44 Topham; pp. 6, 10, 12, 13, 15, 16, 23, 27, 32 Bridgeman Art Library; p. 11 Hulton Archive; pp. 14, 17, 19, 20, 33, 36 AKG; p. 21 Picasso, study for The Family of Saltimbanques, 1905, © Succession Picasso/DACS 2003/Bridgeman Art Library; p. 24 Corbis; p. 25 Picasso, Les Demoiselles d'Avignon, 1907, © Succession Picasso/DACS 2003/Topham; p. 28 Hodder Wayland Picture Library; pp. 30, 38, 39 Popperfoto; p. 31 Picasso, Three Musicians, 1921, © Succession Picasso/DACS 2003/Rex; pp. 34, 40 Rex.

Other acknowledgments
Cover photo of Pablo Picasso in 1973 provided by Topham.
Title page photo of Picasso in his studio in 1935 provided by Rex.

Note to the Reader
Some words are shown in bold, **like this.** You can find out what they mean by looking in the glossary.

Contents

Guernica

The Spanish Civil War had been raging since 1936. In April 1937, bombers sent by Germany to assist the Spanish rebels destroyed the Spanish town of Guernica. When Pablo Picasso, the world-famous artist, heard the news, he was very angry. He began working on a painting he would call *Guernica*.

An old woman stands among the rubble of bombed buildings during the Spanish Civil War.

After decades of traveling to museums around the world, it was not until the 100th anniversary of Picasso's birth, on October 25, 1981, that Guernica was returned to Spain. It now hangs at the Reina Sofía, Spain's national museum of modern art.

"In the panel on which I am working and which I shall call Guernica, and in all my recent works of art, I clearly express my abhorrence [hatred] of the military caste [class] which has sunk Spain in an ocean of pain and death. . . ." Picasso in May 1937.

On a huge canvas, Picasso painted humans and animals that were twisted and broken up into strange shapes. Their mouths were wide open as if they were screaming in agony. He used only black and white paint and shades of gray to paint the scene. When the painting was put on display at the Paris International Exhibition in July 1937, people were stunned. His powerful images said more than words ever could to show that war was a senseless waste of life.

A Spanish Childhood

Pablo Picasso was born at midnight on October 25, 1881, in Málaga, a seaside town in the south of Spain. At first it seemed that he was born dead. This brush with death at the beginning of his life always fascinated Picasso.

An engraving of Málaga from the 1800s. The round white building with the arches is the bullfighting arena.

"When I was a child, my mother said to me, 'If you become a soldier, you'll be a general. If you become a monk you'll end up as the pope.' Instead I became a painter and wound up as Picasso."
Picasso, quoted in *Life with Picasso* by Françoise Gilot.

Picasso's father at age 32. He was a strong influence on Picasso and taught his son about art.

Picasso came from a poor but loving family. His father, José Ruíz Blasco, was a painter and art teacher who often struggled to support his family. His mother, María Picasso López, encouraged her son to become an artist. In 1884 Picasso's sister Lola was born. Another sister, Conchita, was born in 1887, but she died when she was seven years old.

From Picasso's youth, his father took him to watch bullfights in Málaga. Picasso always enjoyed watching the battles between the bull and the brave *toreador* (the Spanish word for bullfighter). The drama of life and death that thrilled him in bullfights would later inspire many of his paintings.

Black-Eyed Boy

Picasso's mother fondly recalled that Picasso could draw before he could speak properly. She also said that his first words were "piz, piz," from lápiz, the Spanish word for pencil. By the time Picasso was nine, his pencil sketches showed that he had far greater drawing ability than other children of the same age. In 1891 the family moved to La Coruña, a province on the north coast of Spain. Picasso's father took a job teaching at the Institute of Fine Arts.

Picasso at age seven. Family and friends often commented on his piercing black eyes, which could see things that other people did not notice.

Picasso's father loved to draw pigeons. Many of Picasso's paintings feature birds, too. Here Picasso and his second wife, Jacqueline, attend an exhibition of his work in Nice in 1961.

"For being a bad student, they would send me to the 'cells.' . . . I loved it when they sent me there, because I could take a pad of paper and draw nonstop." Picasso remembering his school days in La Coruña. From *Picasso: Creator and Destroyer.*

At school Picasso preferred doodling to paying attention in class. He was not very good at math and, later in his life, he claimed that he never learned the alphabet correctly. His talent was for drawing, not writing. In 1892 he began formal art training at the Institute. But in 1895 the family moved to Barcelona. Picasso was only fourteen but his entrance exam to the School of Fine Arts in Barcelona was so outstanding that he was accepted despite his young age.

Taste of Freedom

Throughout his long life, Picasso longed to do things his own way. When he studied at the School of Fine Arts in Barcelona, he soon became fed up with its strict rules. He would often escape the classroom to explore the streets of Barcelona. In October 1897, at the age of sixteen, he enrolled at the prestigious Royal Academy of San Fernando in Madrid.

This painting from the 1800s is of Madrid, where Picasso went to college in 1897.

However, it wasn't long before he was skipping classes so he could wander about Madrid's dark alleys, sketching the scenes that interested him. Picasso preferred to draw what he saw in real life, such as gypsies and beggars, rather than the **classical** subjects taught at the Academy.

In 1899 Picasso returned to Barcelona. His favorite place was a café called El Quatre Gats (The Four Cats). Here Picasso could mingle with other artists, writers, and poets. He sketched the customers and many of his pictures were pinned up on the walls of the café.

Barcelona in the early 1900s. Picasso enjoyed living in Barcelona and socializing with new people who were interested in the arts.

The Magic of Paris

Picasso visited Paris for the first time in October 1900 with his friend, poet Carlos Casagemas. One of Picasso's paintings had been chosen for the Spanish Pavilion at the International Exhibition of 1900, which, for an unknown artist, was a great honor.

Visitors to the International Exhibition of 1900 in Paris may have bought postcards like this one. Many people came to see the Eiffel Tower lit up with electric lights.

*This painting, **Sunday Afternoon on the Island of La Grande Jatte** (1884–1886), is by Georges Pierre Seurat (1859–1891). He developed a technique known as pointillism, in which a whole painting is made up of tiny dots of color.*

In the 1860s the great **Impressionist** painters Claude Monet (1840–1926) and Auguste Renoir (1841–1919) had exhibited in Paris. They had shocked the art world with their new style of painting. For many years they were criticized and lived in poverty. By the 1880s, though, their style had become more popular. Then **Postimpressionist** painters, such as Vincent van Gogh (1853–1890), Paul Gauguin (1848–1903) and Henri de Toulouse-Lautrec (1864–1901), created new ways of painting with thick outlines and bright colors. Though many of these men were not famous until after they had died, they were an inspiration to young artists like Picasso.

Parisian Nights

On October 25, 1899, Picasso celebrated his nineteenth birthday. He and Casagemas had been living in an area of Paris called Montmartre. It was a well-known place for penniless artists and writers to live. The cafés and bars were filled with chattering and laughing people. Music and noise were everywhere. Picasso had met a group of Spanish artists and most nights they went out together. With his boyish good looks and his charming personality, Picasso was always popular with women.

This postcard from 1898 shows a ballroom called Moulin de la Galette. Picasso painted it on his first visit to Paris.

Picasso often copied the style of other painters. Picasso's 1900 painting of the Moulin de la Galette was influenced by Toulouse-Lautrec's 1890 painting, **The Dance at the Moulin Rouge,** *pictured above.*

"Some nights we got to . . . theaters. . . . Here everything is fanfare, full of tinsel and cloth made of cardboard and papier-mâché. . . . Whenever there is light . . . we are in the studio painting and drawing." Casagemas writing about their life in Paris in a letter to a friend in Barcelona. From *Picasso: Creator and Destroyer.*

Life was fun and exciting, but Picasso never forgot why he was in Paris. He continued to sketch and paint and experimented with the bright colors used by van Gogh and Lautrec. His work was noticed by an art dealer named Petrus Manyac who offered him 150 **francs** (approximately $24) a month for his paintings. Picasso accepted the deal, but by Christmas 1899 he was ready to return to his family home in Málaga.

Feeling Blue

A painting of Madrid in 1900 by Enrique Martínez Cubells y Ruíz. Picasso was in Madrid when he heard about the death of his friend Casagemas.

It was wonderful to be back on the Mediterranean coast, but Picasso found himself becoming restless. After just two weeks at home he left and went back to Madrid, where he struggled to survive on the money from Manyac. Then, in February, he heard his friend Casagemas had shot himself in a café in Paris. Picasso was depressed, and the only way he knew how to make himself feel better was to paint. But he still felt unsettled in Madrid, and when he was asked to exhibit his work in Paris, he decided to go back there.

Poor areas of Montmartre, such as the one shown above, were where Picasso got much of his inspiration for his paintings during his Blue Period.

Picasso moved into a **studio** next to the café where Casagemas had killed himself. Once again Picasso was attracted to sketching the loneliness and misery that he saw on the streets of Montmartre. The paintings were sad and haunted because he only used shades of blues, grays, and greens. This time is known as Picasso's Blue Period, and it lasted until 1904.

Struggling to Survive

Picasso's friend, the poet Max Jacob, shown in later life.

Today Picasso's paintings from the Blue Period hang in major museums and art galleries around the world. *Child Holding a Dove, The Tragedy,* and *Woman in a Chemise* can be seen by millions of people. When he painted these pictures, no one would buy them. His depression deepened as he moved from one cheap room to another. Many of his artist friends were poor, too, but Picasso often relied upon their generosity. In 1902 the poet Max Jacob allowed him to move into his tiny room for a few months. They shared everything, even their clothes.

Picasso moved between Paris and Barcelona searching for a better life. In April 1904 he finally decided to make Paris his permanent home. He rented a room in an old piano factory that a friend had called the Bateau Lavoir, which means "Laundry Boat" in French. The rundown building was filled with artists, writers, students, and workers. It was overcrowded and noisy, and Picasso's room was filthy. Yet, out of these surroundings came happiness and success.

The entrance to the Bateau Lavoir in Montmartre looked like this in 1939. Picasso often said his years there were the happiest time of his life.

The Rose Period

Picasso's cluttered room was with filled with junk, furniture, and **canvases.** Before long he had three dogs, a cat, and a white mouse. He made new friends, like the poets Guillaume Apollinaire and André Salmon. His days were spent socializing in cafés and bars. Then at night he worked frantically, producing painting after painting. At this time Picasso met the beautiful Fernande Oliver on the stairs of the Bateau Lavoir. They fell in love, and for the first time in years, he felt happy.

087. — PARIS - Vieux-Montmartre - Cabaret artistique du Lapin Agile   J. H.

Picasso was a regular customer at the cafe Le Lapin Agile, pictured above. In 1905 he painted a picture of himself there called Au Lapin Agile.

Picasso

A sketch for Picasso's 1905 The Family of Saltimbanques, *which shows a group of traveling acrobats.*

As Picasso's spirits rose, the dark blues and greens in his paintings were replaced with reds and pinks. The years 1905 to 1906 are now known as his Rose Period. One of the most famous paintings from this time is *The Family of Saltimbanques*. *Saltimbanque* means "traveling acrobat" in French.

Golden Days

Picasso's paintings were hung next to those of the painter Henri Matisse in 2002 and 2003, in a major exhibition that toured the world. A Picasso self-portrait from 1906 (left) hangs next to a self-portrait by Matisse.

Picasso lived at the Bateau Lavoir for five years. While most artists were eager to exhibit their work, Picasso refused to show his paintings to the public. He could have made money by illustrating magazines, but Picasso believed his talents were too great for this type of work.

"The first picture we had of his . . . was full of grace and delicacy and charm. After that, little by little, his drawing hardened, his line become firmer, his color more vigorous [strong]. . . . " Gertrude Stein describing Picasso's changing style after the Rose Period. From *Picasso: Creator and Destroyer.*

In 1904 Picasso's luck began to change. The art dealer Ambroise Vollard bought 30 of his paintings. Then, in 1905 he met the American brother and sister Leo and Gertrude Stein. They lived in Paris and collected paintings by new artists. They began buying Picasso's paintings and hung them on the walls of their apartment next to the work of other artists, such as the **Postimpressionists** Paul Cézanne (1839–1906) and Henri Matisse (1869–1954). Suddenly, at the age of 25, Picasso's work was in demand and his days as a poor artist were over. But he still wasn't satisfied and he searched for new ways of expressing himself.

Paul Cézanne painted this picture, Rocks, in 1904. His modern style influenced Picasso.

A Shocking Style

In the spring of 1906, Picasso persuaded Gertrude to pose for a portrait. He was able to paint her body, but he couldn't get her face quite right. Overwhelmed by frustration, he left for a vacation in Spain and painted her face from memory when he got back. Her face wasn't a true likeness; it was more like a primitive mask. His friends were critical of the unflattering painting, but Gertrude liked it.

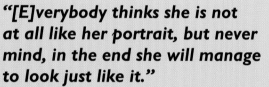

"[E]verybody thinks she is not at all like her portrait, but never mind, in the end she will manage to look just like it."
Picasso's reaction to criticism of his portrait of Gertrude Stein. From *Picasso: Creator and Destroyer.*

Gertrude Stein sits beneath her portrait by Picasso. Many people thought Gertrude looked more like her portrait as she got older.

24

Picasso painted Les Demoiselles d'Avignon in 1907, but it wasn't shown to the public until 1916. It was not until the 1930s that its importance was appreciated.

Picasso was inspired. In the spring of 1907 he gathered his close friends at his **studio** to show them a new painting: *Les Demoiselles d'Avignon*. When he revealed his painting, they were shocked to see five naked women with strange-looking bodies and masklike faces. This revolutionary painting is now recognized as the beginning of modern art.

Invention of Cubism

Picasso continued to paint in the same style as he had with *Les Demoiselles d'Avignon*. He worked closely with the French artist Georges Braque (1882–1963) and together they created a new painting style that would be called **Cubism.** Everyday objects became a collection of cubes and geometric shapes. When Picasso painted a portrait of the art dealer Daniel-Henry Kahnweiler, it was almost impossible to recognize him. Cubism was criticized by many, but it also captured the imaginations of artists around the world.

*Picasso's friend Georges Braque in 1909 at Picasso's **studio**. Picasso described them as being like two rock climbers tied together. He meant that their work was so closely linked that if one of them made a mistake, it would have a direct effect on the other.*

Collectors from around the world were buying Picasso's work, and he had enough money to live well. However, he waited until 1909 before he moved to a luxury apartment in a better part of Paris. He hired a maid, but wouldn't allow her to dust in case it settled on his precious canvases.

"Painting is freedom. If you jump, you might fall on the wrong side of the rope. But if you're not willing to take the risk of breaking your neck, what good is it? You don't jump at all. You have to wake people up." Picasso describing his work. From *Picasso: Creator and Destroyer.*

Picasso in his studio with a sketch for one of his Cubist paintings behind him.

The End of an Era

Parisians gather in the street to watch German planes fly over France during World War I (1914–1918).

Fernande was jealous of the time Picasso spent with Braque, so they broke up in 1912. Picasso then fell in love with Marcelle Humbert. Picasso and Marcelle spent happy vacations in Spain and the south of France, and life seemed good. Braque and Picasso continued to experiment with **Cubism.** They glued pieces of newspaper, wallpaper, rope, and cardboard to their pictures in a style that became known as **collage.** But in 1914 World War I began and life changed for everybody.

Many of Picasso's friends went off to fight. Picasso couldn't join them because he was Spanish and the war did not involve Spain. Then, in 1916, Marcelle died. It was a bleak, lonely time for Picasso. But his spirits were raised when he visited Rome in 1917 to work on the costumes and scenery for the ballet *Parade*. He worked alongside the great ballet **producer** Sergei Diaghilev, his close friend and playwright Jean Cocteau, and composer Erik Satie.

"He is small in stature and built like a bullfighter. His skin is sallow [pale and yellowish] and his wicked black eyes are set close together; the mouth is strong and finely drawn. . . . " A Danish art critic describes Picasso's appearance in 1916. From *A Life of Picasso 1907–1917: The Painter of Modern Life.*

Picasso (left) with Jean Cocteau at a bullfight in Barcelona in 1956. They were close friends until Cocteau's death in 1963.

A Family Man

Picasso and Olga in 1919. For a short while, under Olga's influence, he ordered suits from the best tailors.

In Rome Picasso met a woman who helped him forget the pain of losing Marcelle. Olga Koklova was a ballet dancer in Diaghilev's Russian ballet. They traveled to Madrid and Barcelona together. When they were married in July 1918, many of Picasso's friends thought their marriage was not likely to last.

In the 1921 painting Three Musicians, *Picasso formed figures from blocks of bright colors. Behind the figure on the left is the shape of a dog, which merges with the floor and table.*

"Braque is the wife who loved me most." Picasso often joked that he was closer to his fellow artist and friend Georges Braque than he was to any of his wives. *From Picasso: His Life and Work.*

In November 1918 World War I ended. The newlyweds moved into an elegant house in Paris. Picasso's happiness was reflected in his paintings, such as *Three Musicians* and *Still Life on a Table*. When Picasso's first son, Paolo, was born in 1921, Picasso seemed to have settled down to enjoy family life. Although he was rich, he still preferred to wear ragged clothes, and his **studio** was always messy and full of **canvases** and his collections.

Surrealism by the Sea

During the 1920s the influence of **Cubism** spread to architecture, fashion, and furniture. There were new movements in art, too. **Surrealism** allowed artists to move away from traditional styles. The Spanish surrealist Salvador Dali (1904–1989) painted dreamlike pictures, such as deserts filled with dead trees and melting clocks. Picasso never claimed to belong to any art group, but he was inspired by everything, and continued to produce a huge amount of work.

Picasso stands in front of his paintings in about 1929. Sketches from the Bathers series can be seen scattered on the floor.

These people are enjoying the French coast in 1929. Picasso loved to watch people relaxing and having fun on the beach.

> **"Painting is a blind man's profession. He paints not what he sees, but what he feels, what he tells himself about what he has seen."**
> Picasso talking about his art. From *The New Penguin Dictionary of Modern Quotations.*

Picasso was now middle aged and could afford to spend his summers in luxury by the coast. He enjoyed the calm of the ocean and was inspired by the beach and watching other people at play. In a series of paintings called *Bathers,* he showed how Surrealism had influenced his work. In 1931 he bought a castle built in the 1600s at Boisgeloup, close to Paris. He set up his **studio** in the stables there and began creating metal sculptures made from everyday objects he found around him.

Picasso's Women

As Picasso's friends had predicted, his marriage with Olga did not last. In 1927 he met another woman named Marie-Thérèse Walter. When Marie-Thérèse became pregnant in 1935, Olga left Picasso, taking Paolo with her. Maya, Picasso's daughter with Marie-Thérèse, was born in 1935, but Picasso's relationship with Marie-Thérèse was soon over as well. In 1936 he fell in love with a photographer named Dora Maar.

*Picasso sitting alone in his **studio** in about 1935. Although Picasso loved the company of women, he was often unkind to them.*

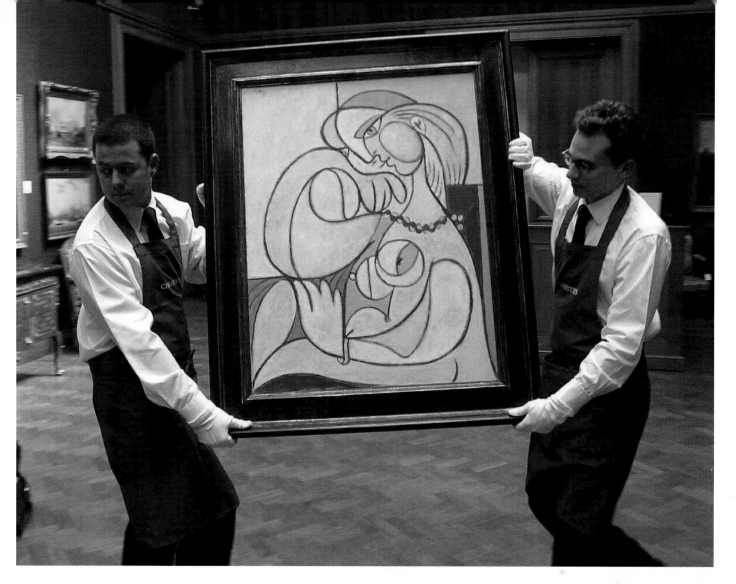

One of Picasso's paintings of Marie-Thérèse Walter arrives at Christie's auction house in London in 2002. It sold for nearly $24 million.

> **"There were five factors that determined his way of life. . . . [They were] the woman with whom he was in love; the poet, or poets, . . . who served as a catalyst; the place where he lived; [his] circle of friends; . . . and the dog who was his inseparable companion. . . ."**
> Dora Maar talking about Picasso in *The New York Review of Books*, 1980.

Women always played a major part in Picasso's life. When he fell in love, it was with passion. The women he loved became the models for his paintings, and he would paint beautiful pictures of them. When he fell out of love with them, his paintings made them look ugly and disgusting. Picasso painted Olga in a **classical** style, but when Picasso painted Marie-Thérèse he chose to use a more **Cubist** style (like the painting in the above photo). The soft lines of this picture show how much he was in love with his subject at that time.

An Ugly War

"I did not paint the war because I am not one of those artists who go looking for a subject like a photographer. But there is no doubt that the war is there in the pictures that I painted then."
Picasso talking about his work during World War II. From *Picasso: Creator and Destroyer.*

Picasso was living in Paris when the **Nazis** occupied the French capital in June 1940. **Picasso was invited** to **emigrate** to America, but he decided to stay. Living in wartime Paris was hard; fuel was **rationed** and art materials were in short supply, but Picasso still painted as much as he could. Many of his paintings were dark and gloomy, and revealed his hatred of the war. They often seemed to suggest the theme of death, as in a series of paintings of animal skulls. Picasso was also sad to have lost so many of his friends in the war, including the poet Max Jacob, who died in a Nazi **concentration camp.**

Adolf Hitler (center) visits occupied Paris on June 28, 1940.

Picasso poses with his arm around one of his life-size sculptures in his Paris studio in 1944.

Picasso hated the Nazis and had friends in the **French Resistance.** He loved telling the story of how a Nazi officer had entered his **studio** and asked him about a photograph of his antiwar painting *Guernica* (in which he depicted the destruction of a Spanish town by Nazi bombers). When the officer asked him if he'd done the picture, Picasso had replied, "No. . . . You did." Many people thought he was very brave to remain in Paris. When the war ended in 1945, Picasso was surprised at how his much reputation had grown.

New Loves

Following the war Picasso lived mainly in the south of France near the sea. His romantic relationships became even more complicated. He received nasty letters from his first wife, Olga; he frequently argued with Dora; and Marie-Thérèse longed for him to return to her. Picasso spent most of his time working in a new style of art called **lithography.** This process allowed an original engraving to be reproduced hundreds of times, which made his work more affordable. While he was working on lithographs, Picasso met and fell in love with a 21-year-old artist named Françoise Gilot.

Picasso holds up one of the plates he has decorated at an exhibition of his work in Paris in 1948.

"One starts to get young at the age of 60 and then it is too late." Picasso in an interview with *The Sunday Times,* from *The New Penguin Dictionary of Modern Quotations.*

In this 1953 photo of Picasso, Françoise, and their two children, Picasso shows how he helped Claude and Paloma learn to draw. They practiced drawing pigeons, just as Picasso had done as a child.

Now in his 60s, Picasso became a father again. In 1947 Françoise gave birth to a baby boy named Claude, and in 1949 she had a girl named Paloma. During these years Picasso experimented with ceramics, often inventing new ways of working in clay. He also began giving his works to museums. In the past, because of the shocking style and subject matter of some of his art, museums hadn't bought his works. Now **curators** were asking Picasso to donate his paintings because they couldn't afford to buy them.

Eye of a Genius

Françoise Gilot and her children had been a source of great happiness and inspiration for Picasso's bright and colorful paintings. But after the birth of Paloma, he seemed to lose interest in his family, and in 1953 Françoise left Picasso. He moved to a large house in the hills above Cannes in the south of France. Picasso had become the first celebrity artist and fans often gathered in front of his home to try to meet him. He preferred a quiet life, so only a select few visitors were invited through the gates into his home.

As he grew older, Picasso rarely left his home except to attend bullfights in Spain.

Picasso with his second wife, Jacqueline, in his studio at his country house, Notre Dame de Vie, in a town just outside Cannes. Behind Picasso is a painting from 1931 called Figures by the Sea.

"Today, as you know, I am famous and very rich. But when I am alone with myself, I haven't the courage to consider myself an artist, in the great and ancient sense of that word. . . . I am only a public entertainer, who understands his age."
Picasso in an interview in *Le Spectacle du monde* in 1962.

Picasso met Jacqueline Roque in 1954 and she became his model for most of his later works. They were married in 1961 and moved to a house outside Cannes where he could concentrate on his work. By now he was experimenting with all kinds of materials for his artwork. His sculptures were often made from old pieces of metal or trash. His ability to see life in everyday objects and turn them into new works of art amazed people.

The Great Master

Even as his paintings were attracting a great deal of attention, Picasso himself preferred to remain in his studio. Although he was 84 when this photograph was taken, he was still working hard.

In the 1960s Picasso's work was exhibited throughout the world. One of the most memorable exhibitions was in 1966 when more than 700 of his works were shown in different galleries in Paris. By this time Picasso had become a **recluse** and did not visit the exhibition. He said he had grown tired of life, and began questioning the meaning of his work. At one point he asked, "Painting, exhibiting—what's it all about?"

Picasso in early 1973, a few months before his death.

"Picasso is what is going to happen and what is happening."
In 1970 the Mexican poet Octavio Paz described the influence that Picasso had on the world of art, showing how his importance continued to be recognized as the years passed.

In his final years, Picasso's eyesight and hearing started to fail. Although he refused to see many of his relatives, including his children, he never lost his creative energy. Later paintings, such as *The Kiss* or *The Couple,* were as original and powerful as his early works. In 1972 he painted his last self-portrait. It was of an old man with a face twisted with pain. Picasso died at his home in Notre Dame de Vie in Mougins, France, on April 8, 1973, at the age of 91.

Picasso's Legacy

Picasso was buried on the grounds of one of his homes, the castle in Vauvenargues in Provence, France. His death was followed by one tragedy after another. On the day of his funeral, his grandson, also named Pablo, drank bleach and died three months later. In 1977 a frail and depressed Marie-Thérèse hanged herself at the age of 68. In 1986 Jacqueline, his last wife, committed suicide as well.

The final resting place of Pablo Picasso is on the secluded grounds of his castle home in Provence. On the day of his burial, it snowed.

"God is really the only other artist. He invented the giraffe, the elephant, and the cat. He has no real style. He just keeps on trying other things." Pablo Picasso in *Life with Picasso.*

The public's fascination with Picasso continues. Exhibitions of his work still draw huge crowds.

Picasso was a man of many **contradictions.** He was a Spaniard who adopted France as his homeland. He was charming and witty, but he could also be cruel and was often depressed. He founded a new movement in art called **Cubism,** but he disliked being labeled as any particular kind of artist. He became a multimillionaire, but he preferred to dress in ragged clothing. Art critics are divided about his work. Was he a genius or merely in the right place at the right time? Whatever we think of Pablo Picasso, his life, and his work, he has become one of the most admired and influential artists that ever lived.

45

Glossary

canvas cloth used as a surface for painting

catalyst something that causes change

classical art style that borrows from the traditions of ancient Greece and Rome

collage art style that uses a mixture of materials, such as paper cutouts

concentration camp prison camp to which Jews and members of many other groups were sent by the Nazis before and during World War II

contradictions opposing qualities or ideas

Cubism style of art in which images are formed from many geometric shapes

curator planner of museum exhibits

emigrate to move to another country

engraving design that is cut into metal, wood, or glass

francs money used in France before 1999

French Resistance group in France that secretly worked to resist the Nazis during World War II

Impressionist painter of the late 1800s who used colors and textures to give an impression of a scene rather than a realistic depiction of it

lithography process of making prints

Nazi supporter of Adolf Hitler, the leader of Germany from 1933 to 1945

Postimpressionist painter of the late 1800s and early 1900s who favored an even less realistic style of art than the Impressionists

producer organizer of public events

rationed shared out equally

recluse person who prefers to live alone

studio room where an artist works

Surrealism movement in art and literature in the early 1900s, in which artists used bizarre, dreamlike images in their works

Further Information

Books to Read

Langley, Andrew. *Pablo Picasso.* Chicago: Raintree, 2002.

Mason, Antony. *In the Time of Picasso: The Foundation of Modern Art.* Brookfield, Conn.: Millbrook, 2002.

Sources of Quotes

Andrews, Robert. *The New Penguin Dictionary of Modern Quotations.* London: Penguin, 2001.

Gilot, Françoise, and Carlton Lake. *Life with Picasso.* New York: McGraw-Hill, 1964.

Huffington, Arianna S. *Picasso: Creator and Destroyer.* New York: Simon and Schuster, 1988.

Penrose, Roland. *Picasso: His Life and Work.* Berkeley: University of California, 1981.

Richardson, John. *A Life of Picasso 1907–1917: The Painter of Modern Life.* London: Jonathan Cape, 1996.

Date Chart

October 25, 1881 Pablo Ruíz Blasco Picasso is born in Málaga, Spain.

1891 Picasso's family moves to La Coruña on the Atlantic coast of Spain. Picasso begins to study under his father.

1895 Picasso's family moves to Barcelona. Picasso attends the School of Fine Arts.

1897 Picasso attends the Royal Academy of San Fernando in Madrid.

October 1900 Picasso visits Paris for the first time with his friend Carlos Casagemas.

1901–1904 Picasso's Blue Period.

1905–1906 Picasso's Rose Period. He falls in love with Fernande Oliver.

1907 Picasso paints *Les Demoiselles d'Avignon,* the painting now considered to be the beginning of modern art. He works with Georges Braque and experiments with a style of painting that is later called Cubism.

1908 Picasso and Braque's Cubist paintings are exhibited in Paris.

1912 Picasso and Braque experiment with collage. Picasso breaks up with Fernande and falls in love with Marcelle Humbert.

1914 World War I begins.

1917 Picasso works with Jean Cocteau, Erik Satie, and Sergei Diaghilev on a production of the ballet *Parade.* He travels to Rome and meets Olga Koklova.

July 1918 Picasso marries Olga Koklova. **November** World War I ends.

1921 Picasso's first son, Paolo, is born.

1935 Marie-Thérèse gives birth to Picasso's first daughter Maya. Picasso and his wife, Olga, separate.

1936 The Spanish Civil War begins.

April 1937 The bombing of the town of Guernica in Spain inspires Picasso to paint his great antiwar painting *Guernica.*

September 1939 World War II begins; death is the subject of many of Picasso's paintings. He meets Françoise Gilot and works on lithographs.

1940 The Nazis occupy Paris.

1947 Françoise Gilot gives birth to Picasso's second son, Claude. Picasso moves to the south of France.

1949 Françoise Gilot gives birth to Picasso's second daughter, Paloma.

1953 Picasso and Françoise break up.

1954 Picasso meets Jacqueline Roque.

1961 Picasso marries Jacqueline Roque.

1966 Over 700 of Picasso's works are displayed in Paris in honor of his 85th birthday.

1971 Picasso becomes the first living artist to have his works on display at the Louvre in Paris.

April 8, 1973 Picasso dies in his house in Notre Dame de Vie, Mougins, at age 91.

1980 A major exhibition of his work is held at the Museum of Modern Art in New York City.

2002 A major exhibition of the works of Picasso and Henri Matisse begins its tour of the world.

Index

All text in **bold** refers to pictures as well as text.